Leaming's Run Gardens

How It All Began

By Emily Heath Aprill

Thomas Leaming and the Thomas Leaming House

Leaming's Run Gardens
How It All Began

by **Emily Heath Aprill**
wife of Jack Aprill
the designer and owner of
Leaming's Run Gardens

1845 Historic Route 9 in Swainton,
Cape May County, New Jersey
Exit 13 on the Garden State Parkway

Over 20 acres of spectacular flowers, ferns,
lawn and ponds displayed in 25 gardens.

**Leaming's Run Gardens and Colonial Farm
has the distinction of being
the largest annual garden in the United States, and
one of the top 10 gardens in the East.**

1st printing July 1997

ISBN 0-9641387-3-5

Printed in the United States of America
Garden State Printing
Fairfield, New Jersey

Skip Gladue, Editor
Helen-joe Owens, Production Director
Joan Berkey, Research

Photos by Emily Aprill and Joan Berkey

To Jack
with love and much admiration,
for having the vision to create our gardens.

To our sons and their families
who enrich our lives every day:
Glenn and Sandy
Roy, Linda, Aaron and Jared
Tim, Graceanne, Jason, Triston and Morgan Ann
and our dear Gregg.

To my sister and brother,
Bernice Collerd and Bob Heath,
with love.

And, in loving memory of my mother
Clara Bullard Heath.

Other Books About Leaming's Run

Gardening Without Work

Garden Myths, Misconceptions
and Old Wives Tales

Feeding Hummingbirds Nature's Way

all by Jack Aprill

Contents

In the Beginning 1

Early Years 5

Dried Flower Shop 6

Designing and Creating the Gardens 9

Cinnamon Fern 11

The Bamboo Stand 15

Stocking our Ponds 16

The Colonial Farm 19

Log Cabin 20

Barn and Animals 22

Naming the Gardens 24

Keeping Animals at Bay 26

Hummingbirds 27

The Peacock 28

Caretakers of History 29

History of Thomas Leaming 31

Chronology of the Property 32

Architecture 36

Epilogue

The Leaming Gravestones 38

Preface

Over the years so many people have asked Jack and me why we made a garden and how we actually did it. This book tells our story of finding our house with fifty acres, starting the dried flower shop and creating the gardens.

We used all our own resources including funds to make and maintain the gardens. We have never relied on federal, state or county funds. We wanted to do this on our own and we did.

Emily Aprill

In the Beginning

*I don't believe in fate as a rule but finding this
beautiful old house with fifty acres, I believe was fate.*

We had been transferred to Cape May County, and whenever we were transferred we always rented first and then looked for a home to buy. One day when Jack forgot his briefcase at the office, our little boy Tim and I rode to Cape May with Jack to get the briefcase. While riding down Route 9 I saw a for sale sign. "Oh, Jack I love that house," I exclaimed. It was New England style with a tall spruce tree in the front and a huge maple by the back door. The house was sitting on a small rise which also appealed to me.

Jack agreed saying, "It is nice, I like it too."

The next time Jack went to the office he stopped in to see the house. How well I remember when he came home and told me all about it . . . its wide pine floorboards, antique doors with H and L hinges and old latches, the old barn and root cellar. We went to see it together the very next day.

I just felt so at home there and knew it would be perfect for our family. When the owner told us the house also included fifty acres, she said it almost apologetically. At the time we had three sons — Glenn, Roy and Tim later to be joined by Gregg — and thought it would be wonderful for the boys to have these wooded acres in which to explore and roam.

There were about two acres cleared around the house and barn and the rest of the acreage was wooded with trees of OAK, HOLLY, CEDAR, PINE, SWEET GUM and LOW and HIGH BUSH BLUEBERRIES. We decided to buy the house that very day.

The Thomas Leaming House Today

Wherever we lived Jack always planted beautiful flower and vegetable gardens. Having been raised on a farm, Jack now was delighted to have room for vegetable and flower gardens, sheep and chickens.

The timing worked out just right as we had a year's lease on the house we were renting and the owners of this house were building a new one. Since this was November, the boys would be able to finish the school year where they'd started. At this point in our lives we had moved ten times and sometimes Glenn would have to change school in midyear which is a hard thing for a child to do.

A Piece of History

We also learned that our house — the Thomas Leaming House, built in 1706, — was one of the original houses in Cape May County. Also, it is the only remaining whaler's house in the county.

The second part of this book is about the history of the house and property, which remained in the Leaming family until 1926, when Annie Leaming died. Annie never married. She taught piano and violin and would walk miles to her students. Her carpetbag, which she carried on these walks, is on display at the Cape May County Museum along with her shell collection and a mounted rattlesnake which was killed on this property, or so they say. We've never seen or heard of this phenomenon; this is not rattlesnake country.

Years ago I was fortunate enough to meet a few elderly ladies who knew Annie; in fact, some took music lessons from her. They told me that she and her sister Emma were in love with the same man. When her sister was chosen to marry him, and then they built the Victorian house across the street from the Leaming house, Annie vowed she'd make them ashamed of her. It's been said that Annie was not very clean personally and she kept pigs and chickens in the kitchen.

When she died in 1926 she had $10,000 and stated in her will she wanted all the money spent on her funeral. I doubt that happened. She is buried in a Cape May Court House Cemetery on Route 9. There is a newspaper article about her death at the Cape May County Historical Society Museum.

After Annie's death, the house was bought and rented out over the next twenty or so years. When Lee and Richard Hutton (the former owners) purchased the property they told us the house and yard were overrun with HONEYSUCKLE, VINCA and ENGLISH IVY. As could be expected, the house was in bad repair. Along with painting and general repairs, the Huttons put in plumbing and heating at that time and also refinished the pine floors.

The house construction is oak and cedar beams with cedar siding. The outside of the house was covered with stucco at some point, probably because the siding was in poor repair.

Although I wish the cedar siding were still exposed, the stucco is wonderful insulation; our house is cool in the summer and warmer in the winter.

When asbestos shingles came into vogue in the 1940s, many of the old houses were covered with them. Later when people bought these early houses to restore, they removed the asbestos shingles to expose the beautiful old cedar siding. Soon they realized there was no insulation; the wind whistled through the siding. They then had to have insulation blown in. At least our stucco covering spared us all that.

As I mentioned before, we have a tall SPRUCE in our front yard and a huge SUGAR MAPLE by the back door, (SUGAR MAPLES are not indigenous to this area). Jack read somewhere that the early settlers planted these two kinds of trees, the SPRUCE near the front door and the MAPLE by the back door, to ward off goblins. For whatever reason, we are delighted to have such beautiful examples of each tree.

Early Years

We bought this house in 1957 and have lived happily here. The boys enjoyed playing and exploring in the woods, and especially liked the run stream. (On early maps this was named Uncle Aaron's run stream; Aaron was Thomas Leaming's brother).

They floated wooden boats from Sandy Land (their name for a special place on the western end of the stream) all the way to Route 9 where the stream enters a pipe under the road to continue on its way to the meadows, wetlands, bay and ocean.

Jack and the boys made some paths through the woods as we all enjoyed walks there, even in winter. I especially remember the winter weekend we had a hot dog roast under the pines where the Colonial Farm is now, with blueberry pie a la mode for dessert.

Dried Flower Shop

A few years after we bought our house, a friend of mine and I were on an Old Homes Tour. At one of the houses there was an arrangement of dried flowers on the hearth. I casually mentioned to her that Jack grew a lot of dried flowers.

"Oh, Emily, you should open a shop," she said. She had just returned from a trip to Williamsburg where she had purchased a large box of dried flowers at a very high price. This must have been the right time in my life to think this was an interesting idea.

We have an antique building beside our home called a "cellar" according to the research done on the house. It is only 10 feet by 10 feet. This was to be my shop. What fun it was to fix up this little building.

Earlier, while living here, the boys used this building as a playhouse at times and Glenn and Roy also used it to raise quail for a 4-H project. Baby quail are quite small, not much bigger than one's thumb. I remember so well when a king snake got into the quail pen, and dined on 10 quail; you could count the bumps.

We decided to open the shop the following year. Much had to be done. Dried flower seeds had to be bought. Jack started the seeds in our greenhouse first and transplanted the plants to the garden behind the barn. He grew STRAW FLOWERS, BABY'S BREATH, NIGELA, STATICE SINUATA, BUNNY TAILS, COCKSCOMB, and LARKSPUR just to name a few. It's a long process from planting seeds to dried flowers. We also picked wild materials such as BROWN BURR, PEARLY EVERLASTING and JOE PYEWEED.

All was made ready in the shop by the following July and a sign was hung by the road, Emily Aprill's Dried Flower Shop. What fun! At that time there were quite a few beautiful antique shops along Route 9. Women on a day's outing would come and visit these shops and they came to mine.

We didn't advertise and the customers came, slowly at first, but that was fine as we had a family to raise.

We made flower arrangements and also sold dried materials for our customers to do their own. Our flower arrangements were the same kind colonial housewives used to add color and charm to their homes. We designed Williamsburg-type arrangements including finger vases. Because we raised our own flowers and dried them ourselves, our customers were surprised and pleased with the freshness and bright colors of our dried flowers. (I think we've all seen dried arrangements in shops and department stores that are colorless, dull and drab.)

We learned a lot over the years as to when to pick the flowers; too early and they don't open properly, too late and they went to seed. I've had the shop for over 28 years and I never tire of working with dried flowers. I remember my first customer as if it were yesterday. Her name is Elizabeth Errickson, and she spent $25. That was exciting. She still comes every year when she's vacationing in Avalon, and it's always a pleasure to see my old friend.

My mother Clara Heath made hand-sewn quilts. Usually they were given to the family; she made a baby quilt for each new grandchild and great grandchild. When my shop opened she was delighted to sell some of her quilts, and was so pleased when my customers bought them.

Some wrote her a note of thanks and appreciation for her work. She had always been a housewife and worked hard raising seven children. Now she had a new career making money on her own. She was thrilled. I also remember when an interior decorator from Philadelphia bought five quilts for her own shop. I always was pleased to have mother's quilts in my shop, they added charm and color. Some of my customers still ask about my mother and still have her quilts. She died in 1993, almost 102 years of age.

The success of the dried flower shop enabled Jack to take the road less traveled by, and make his garden.

Designing and Creating the Gardens

Jack and I had always visited gardens whenever we traveled. We found the southern gardens were mostly AZALEA blooming in the spring and not much in bloom in summer and fall. Jack would say I'd love to see a garden featuring annual flowers that would have blooms in abundance through summer and fall as the gardens surrounding our house did. I recall so well the day Jack came to me and said he'd like to make a garden in our woods planted only with annuals.

Jack said when he closed his eyes he could picture the whole garden in his mind even the colors. Then he drew a map of the design on paper. It seemed like such a huge project to me, I didn't know how it could be done. However, Jack had every confidence we could do it with planning and hard work. His enthusiasm was contagious. After much discussion we decided to do it. . . no small feat. What I meant earlier when I said fate had a hand in our finding this house with acreage, was that if we hadn't had all this land available with beautiful woods, located on Route 9, we could not even contemplate having a garden the size we anticipated in such a good location.

Aside from wanting to have a beautiful colorful garden, we wanted to preserve this special area and make an island of peace and beauty for all to share and enjoy. Everyone is so busy, and life gets hectic and stressful at times, we all need a place to go to soothe our souls and enjoy God's beauty. We hoped our garden would be that place for our visitors and for us as well.

Our garden is in the middle of the East coast holly belt, an area where holly grows as a solid understory in the forest.

We also have WILD MAGNOLIA with its delightful fragrance, SWAMP AZALEA that has an aroma of cloves and SWEET PEPPER BUSH too. The aromas in June are glorious, especially when the MULTI-FLORA ROSE, HONEYSUCKLE and MAGNOLIAS blend their special scents.

Among my favorite gardens are The Yellow, The Blue and White, the English Cottage, The Pink, and The 150-foot Serpentine.

Cinnamon Fern

Our property also contained a large area of CINNAMON FERN. We felt they were so special and beautiful they just had to be preserved. They reach heights of almost seven feet in the spring and are lush and verdant green. After we opened our gardens, a woman from the New York Natural Museum paid us a visit and identified sixteen different kinds of fern. The CINNAMON FERN is the most abundant. We were also told by the Pennsylvania Fern Society that our fernery is likely to be one of the largest CINNAMON FERN areas in the country.

The gardens also have a wild plant called the SWAMP PINK (common for *Helonias bullata*) which is on the endangered plant list. *Taylor's Garden Encyclopedia* describes it as "a native spring flowering tuberous herb with pink or purplish flowers in long stemmed racemes." Our SWAMP PINKS have been examined and photographed by naturalists over the years. When we first lived here, my sons used to pick these unusual flowers for me when they bloomed in the spring. Of course we were unaware at that time they were endangered.

Because we started with virgin woodland making the gardens was quite a challenge. Ours would be natural with paths through the wooded areas to 25 different color-coordinated gardens and lawns in a design our visitors could copy in their own yards if they wished.

Part of our property was a swampy area. We had our ponds dug there as we felt that water ponds would add so much to the garden design.

We were very fortunate to find a man with a crane and time to dig the ponds. One pond was made by the intended serpentine garden and gazebo at water's edge. (We decided on a serpentine garden after seeing the brick serpentine fence designed by Thomas Jefferson at the University of Virginia where Glenn was getting his master's degree.) This is the larger pond about one-quarter of an acre. We had a smaller one dug about 300 feet from the large one.

One never thinks about the huge quantities of dirt made when a pond is dug. We only visualized this charming water scene. We found the top three feet or so was black peat soil and the rest was beach sand. Did this mean the ocean reached this far at one time? All this rich peat soil was used in the gardens and the sand was used on the paths.

While the ponds were being dug, our next step was to have the areas cleared where the gardens would be. We hired a bulldozer for this purpose. Trees were cut down first and the logs saved to build the planned Colonial Farm. Large holes were dug and the tree stumps buried in each garden area. A few of the gardens didn't have trees and were much easier to deal with. All this took the better part of a fall and winter, weather permitting, and allowing for machinery break-downs. Meanwhile the parking area had to be cleared as well.

Jack made all the garden paths by hand because bulldozers do more damage than needed.

Our son Roy cleared the small bushes first with a machine called a bush hog, similar to a large lawn mower. This was a great help. Sand from the ponds was then used to smooth the paths. The sand was brought to the paths from the pond area with our garden tractor and wagon. We placed sand on the paths in front of the tractor and drove over the sand smoothing it down, and so on.

All this took a long time and was not worked on every day. The garden areas had to be well-spaded, the soil tested and treated with lime to get the proper pH so it would become conditioned to grow plants. Irrigation pipes were laid so there would be water available when needed.

Some summers in our area produce very little rainfall. It is essential that we have a good water supply at all times. The water for the irrigation system is pumped from our ponds.

Sod was laid in the lawn areas around the individual gardens. Our son Tim had worked on a sod farm and was a great help in cutting and laying the sod properly. The sod, delivered at the end of the garden driveway, then was taken by the garden tractor to each garden. We did sow some grass seed, especially along the 150-foot-long Serpentine.

When Glenn was in the eighth grade we built a greenhouse dug into the ground where we grew GERANIUMS and plants to sell to help with his college costs. The glass for the greenhouse came from Jack's father's cold frames when he farmed in the 1930s.

We still use this greenhouse to plant our seeds, starting some in February. When large enough, the seedlings are then moved to cold frames to make room for more seeds to be planted. We plant 280 packets of seed each season. Since our garden is planted with annuals there are changes with the seasons, different flowers are in bloom in May and June, others in July and August and so on.

Jack devised a system of gardening using grass clippings for mulch. This system does not require weeding or fertilizing the gardens because the grass clippings smother the weeds and then decompose which enriches the soil. Jack has written two books on gardening describing his special gardening techniques: *Gardening Without Work* and *Myths, Misconceptions and Old Wives Tales*.

The Bamboo Stand

Our visitors, especially our Oriental ones, are always surprised and pleased to see our large stand of BAMBOO. We have our son Glenn to thank for this BAMBOO. While he was living in Charlottesville, Va. he brought a BAMBOO plant home for us in the back of his pickup truck. Traveling that way, the plant arrived in poor condition but, as you can see, it has thrived and flourished.

There is a saying that once you have BAMBOO you can never get rid of it. It is such a unique plant, in the grass family actually. It spreads underground in a long root that sends up shoots every so often that resemble a fat ASPARAGUS.

BAMBOO is very prolific and spreads rapidly. We have a machete to cut some shoots that pop up in unwanted places, such as the gardens, lawns and even in the hard packed garden paths. BAMBOO is a very strong, fast-growing plant sometimes growing three feet in one day to about fifty feet upon maturity. Our area is about the farthest north this kind of BAMBOO will grow. Even our usually mild winters here sometimes put stress on the BAMBOO.

One year we had a bad ice storm that clung to the leaves (BAMBOO is not deciduous) and we lost quite a few plants but in the spring they rejuvenated and were as good as new. Our BAMBOO stand is one of my favorite places in the gardens — it's cool, quiet and peaceful.

Stocking Our Ponds

When our ponds (which are about ten feet deep in some places) were dug, we discovered they were part of a large underground lake. The water, supplied by underground springs, remains cold in the summer and seldom freezes in the winter.

Therefore, it was important that a balance of life be established in the ponds. Jack went to a neighbor's pond and caught about fifteen large blue gill fish to put in our ponds. Because it was spring, the water was warm only near the surface. The fish stayed there most of the time. Having been recently dug, the ponds offered the fish no protection from predators. In a few days ospreys caught all our fish. We then realized that the ponds would need some growth to provide protection for the fish.

Jack went to a local stream and got some wild WATER LILIES and wild IRIS and planted them in the ponds. They were just growing well when muskrats came from the salt meadows by way of our stream and ate all the WATER LILIES. We were back where we started: no fish and no WATER LILIES. We found stocking our ponds with fish and vegetation was not as easy as we had thought, especially near the ocean with all its sea birds.

However, nature helped us in other ways. Ducks began to land in the ponds and brought with them BLADDER WART entangled on their feet. BLADDER WART is a water weed that grows in the acid waters of southern New Jersey. It quickly established itself and provided protection for the new fish we had put in the ponds. We also added more WATER LILIES. The muskrats were unable to swim through the BLADDER WART without getting entangled and the WATER LILIES survived also.

We noticed that the large fish survived but the small fish didn't. Our son Glenn, who had majored in marine biology, suggested that the death of the baby fish might be due to excessive acidity of the water. We limed the ponds, increasing the pH, and the baby fish survived. The increased pH also helped to control the BLADDER WART. We now have a large population of fish.

Our ponds have a peat bottom and support a greater number of fish than rock or clay-bottomed ponds. The rich soil causes the rapid growth of minute creatures on which the baby fish feed. Our visitors, many of whom live in rock or clay areas, often feel our water is polluted because it is not crystal clear. What they don't understand is that the healthier the water is the more life it sustains. Between the peat bottom and the animal growth, our pond is just the opposite of what most people tend to think it should be.

The water is very pure, there are no houses or pollutants near our pond. Fortunately for us the church owns all the land south of the gardens and the north and west is now protected in a county open land preservation program. Our ponds are now a perfectly balanced home for their inhabitants. There are now about fifteen kinds of fish in the ponds; they are difficult to see because they are wild and remain hidden as much as possible. We have perch, large mouth bass, walleyed pike, calico bass, sunfish, large head minnows, orange minnows, eels, shiners and catfish to name some. We also purchased some koi. They help control the ALGAE and also have a beautiful color. Our sons Gregg and Roy and our grandsons Aaron and Jared have added fish to our ponds over the years.

The ponds have been a great deal of pleasure. A pair of mallard ducks come every spring to make a nest and raise their young. Although they tend to hide when someone approaches, we did see them on several occasions. Ducklings are especially vulnerable to preditators (snapping turtles from the water and birds of prey from the air). I was surprised and delighted to see them all again, almost fully grown. That was a lovely sight.

One year an otter came and spent a week with us; otters are so much fun to watch. A beautiful blue heron comes almost every morning to catch a fish, or two if he's lucky.

And, we now have beautiful water lilies in abundance that rival Monet's at his garden in Givinchy.

The Colonial Farm

"In July 1674 I (Thomas Leaming) was born in South Hampton, Long Island. When I was 18 years of age (1692) I came to Cape May; and that winter had a sore fit of fever and flux. The next summer I went to Philadelphia with my father, (Christopher) who was lame with a withered hand, which held him until his death.

"The winter following I went a WHALING, and we got eight whales, and five of them we drove to the Hoarskills (Lewistown, Delaware) and we went to cut them up and staid a month. The first day of May we came back to Cape May and my father was very sick; and the third day, 1695, departed this life, at the house of Shamgar Hand.

"Then I went to Long Island, staid that summer and in the winter I went a whaling again, and made a great voyage; and in 1697 I worked for John Reeves all summer, and in the winter I went a whaling again.

"In 1698, worked for John Crafford, and on my own land; and that fall had a sore fit of sickness, at Harry Stites and in the year 1700 I lived at my own plantation and worked for Peter Corson. I was married in 1701; and in 1703 I went to Cohansie and fetched brother Aaron. In 1706 I built my house. Samuel Matthews took a horse from me, worth 7 pounds, because I could not train (for the militia because of religious beliefs); In 1707 we made the county road."

After reading this wonderful excerpt from Thomas Leaming's diary, Jack spent the better part of a winter doing research at the Cape May County Museum and at the County Court House. Whaling was such a big part of life in the late 1600s and early 1700s, we decided to build a colonial farm that would tell the story of a whaler's life in that time.

Log Cabin

The first structure Jack built was a log cabin, the temporary shelter Thomas might have used before building his house in 1706. This is a Swedish type log home which Jack copied from the log granary in Greenwich, N.J. which is an original log building; and he also studied the original log house in Gibbstown. Those are the only two remaining log buildings erected by the Swedes who settled that area.

Jack and the Log Cabin

People always ask why we used cement for chinking between the logs. They seem to think cement wasn't used this early in time. That is not true. When Jack and I visited Europe we were shown ancient buildings, including the Roman aqueduct, that used cement.

Our cabin included a large fireplace used for cooking and heat, also an outdoor bake oven. Trees were cut in the area and the straight ones used on the buildings and the less desirable ones used for fences.

Our cabin has one room and appears to depict hardships. In truth, because of whaling the Leamings were very wealthy as is indicated in the second part of this book from the research done by Joan Berkey. Aside from a kitchen garden, fruit trees and wild berries there was an abundance of fish, clams and oysters ready for the taking from the nearby ocean and bay. In addition, herbs were grown for fragrances, to enhance foods, and for medicinal purposes. Often fragrant herbs were thrown on the floor to be walked on to refresh the home. We grow all kinds of vegetables in the kitchen garden, joined with herbs by the cabin door. We also grow sample crops of TOBACCO, COTTON and BROOM CORN.

Barn and Animals

Our barn and the goose house were built next. Jack copied the barn from Eric Sloan's *An Age of Barns*. If you love old barns, this is a wonderful book to read. The upper portion of our barn was used to dry TOBACCO. TOBACCO could have been a cash crop because it was in demand and easily shipped. The bottom part of the barn and adjacent shed were used to shelter animals, such as cows, sheep, chickens and geese.

Our chickens are mostly rare breeds corresponding to the type of chickens brought to the colonies by the early settlers. All the animals on our farm are special to us and are well fed and cared for. (We don't eat them, either.)

We find it amusing, especially in the fall, when people ask about the turkeys, and we reply, "No, we don't eat them for Thanksgiving." The smoke house was used for smoking meats and fish, and was an important way of preserving food for winter.

The Corn Crib and Smokehouse

Building the Barn

All our roof shingles were hand split oak. At first, Jack wanted to be authentic and use an old-time tool to split the shingles but it was so time-consuming he borrowed Roy's wood splitter to do the job. In colonial days most of the family members were called on to make shingles during spare moments.

The Finished Barn

23

Naming the Gardens

Choosing a name was a hard decision and required much thought. Because history is such an interesting part of this property and the run stream is named on the earliest maps of this land, we chose to call the gardens Leaming's Run.

The year before the gardens were opened twenty years ago, Jack planted the whole garden as a trial run to make sure it would look just as he had planned it should. We had been working on the gardens for five years.

When we told people we were going to open the gardens to the public, most said, "What, are you crazy? You're going to deal with the public, why they'll pick your flowers and ruin the gardens with litter." We really didn't believe this would be true. In fact, one of the things we most enjoy is meeting the really wonderful people who thank us for making the gardens.

They have never littered and the only flowers that are picked on occasion are nearly spent blooms people will bring into my shop for identification.

After the gardens were opened, my little flower shop was just too small. We moved the shop into the old barn and renamed it "The Cooperage." (Thomas Leaming, made barrels for whale oil which were shipped to England.)

I really hated to move from my little shop, but was glad the gardens were bringing enough visitors to make the move necessary. We are fortunate and grateful that our son Gregg decided to work with us in the gardens.

While in high school, he worked each summer here, using the techniques Jack had developed. He is now our manager and we couldn't get along without him.

The Cooperage, Emily's Flower Shop

The busiest time for us is when we plant the gardens in late April and early May. We have to be very careful and wait until the threat of a late frost is over. Some springs we do have some frost damage and have to replant some flowers. Working every day, planting usually takes up to three weeks.

When you deal with nature you have to take what's given you. Each year there are different challenges. Some summers we have a drought and have to irrigate every night from closing until dark and again from first light until opening. Other years we get too much rain and it is hard on the flower blooms. We have to close some days as some of the paths flood. We are lucky we have wonderful sandy loam soil here which drains quickly.

Keeping Animals at Bay

We have had to fence in the entire gardens with eight feet of barbed wire and stock fence to keep out herds of deer. If five or six deer make a visit, they can really devastate the gardens. We can't really blame them for wanting to get into the gardens as all those lush plants are really inviting.

Over the years we've tried about every method we've heard about to keep the deer at bay. Bars of soap hung on the fence is one theory that really doesn't help much. Some products like deer repellent are too time-consuming and costly for our large gardens especially because they have to be re-applied after each rain.

Raccoons are another problem for us and our chickens. Every once in awhile, even though we have the chickens all fenced in, a raccoon will get into the chicken pen and kill some. A raccoon's front paws are almost like human hands. If it perseveres long enough, a raccoon can get the chicken wire loose. This happens mostly in the spring when raccoons have their young.

Hummingbirds

Another surprising and delightful event takes place in our gardens in August. Hummingbirds come and usually stay through mid-September, although occasionally they leave the very end of August. Perhaps it is the weather that tells them they'd better be on their way to sunnier climes.

They visit our garden in great numbers because of the large variety of annuals. Their favorites are the CARDINAL FLOWER and the SCARLET CYPRESS VINE.

The hummingbirds are wonderful to behold and our visitors are always pleased and excited to see them. Incidentally, the flowers also attract large numbers and varieties of butterflies.

Last year on one of my usual early walks in the garden I saw a hummingbird bathing in the dewdrops on a large grape leaf. It was a delightful sight. Although it lasted only a few seconds, I'll always remember it and smile to myself each time I recall it.

The Peacock

People may think it's strange that a colonial farm
would have a peacock.

One evening about three or four years ago, Jack looked out of the kitchen window and saw a beautiful peacock in our driveway. He called me to come and see, but when we went outside, it went behind our barn. We thought that would be the last we would see of the peacock.

When Gregg went to the Colonial Farm the next day, there was the peacock right at home. We let him run free for a long time, but found when the kitchen garden was planted outside the cabin door, the peacock just loved the tender LETTUCE.

We then put him in a pen to save the LETTUCE and other plants, and also for his own safety. He's so beautiful and graceful and such a lovely sight when he fans his glorious tail feathers in the sunlight. We don't know where he came from but we're so happy he decided to live here with us.

Incidentally, the gardens have been featured in *Architectural Digest* and *New Choices* magazines. Articles about the gardens have appeared in all the major east coast newspapers including *The Washington Post, The New York Times, The Philadelphia Inquirer*, and more.

Caretakers of History

The Thomas Leaming house, built in 1706, is the only remaining whaler's house in Cape May County. It's always been a pleasure for us to live in this old house. I feel we are the caretakers and have tried to treat it with the respect it deserves, although raising four sons here, it wasn't always easy to do.

I've really loved living here and hope to spend the rest of my days right here. One of my favorite views is to look out the bedroom window at the beautiful old SUGAR MAPLE and see a nest of robins, a downy woodpecker or a squirrel leaping from limb to limb. I wonder how many other women have looked at this same view over the years.

When you think of all the history that has taken place in this old house over two hundred and ninety years, it would be wonderful if the walls could talk: marriages, births, deaths, sicknesses, Christmases, tears and laughter. The daily life of its inhabitants, would be so interesting.

I am so grateful to have lived here for all these years.

Creating our gardens has been one of the best decisions of our lives. Although a great deal of work is involved, we thoroughly enjoy it and look forward to opening every spring.

One of the many delights of our garden is meeting so many wonderful people. We've had visitors from every state and many foreign countries.

What pleases me the most is when people come to me and tell me how peaceful and relaxed they feel after visiting the gardens. Some tell me it's like a religious experience for them.

I understand how they feel, as I feel that way too.

A History of Thomas Leaming
and
The Thomas Leaming House

Compiled from Research by Joan Berkey

The Thomas Leaming House, built in 1706, is significant in the area of exploration/settlement as it represents the settling and development of Cape May County in the late 18th/early 19th centuries, and in the area of maritime history as the residence of Thomas Leaming, a prominent Cape May County whaler, landowner and judge who built the house in 1706 and lived there until his death in 1723.

The house also is architecturally significant as an early example of New England-influenced heavy timber frame construction, a kind of construction that was common in New Jersey, but has rarely survived. Of those that remain in New Jersey, Cape May County probably holds most of the surviving examples, although few have been identified or extensively studied.

Within the county, the Thomas Leaming House is the earliest documented example of this method of construction and is, to date, the only extant pioneering whaler's house to be identified on the Cape May peninsula.

Chronology of the Property

In April 1694, Christopher Leaming I (1635-1695) purchased 204 acres of land on the "south-side" of the Cape May peninsula from the West Jersey Society. The tract of land stretched one mile from northwest to northeast and was one-quarter-mile deep from northwest to southwest. Located on the upper part of the peninsula, it had frontage on Stites Sound, a body of water between the mainland and the barrier island of Seven Mile Beach (later Avalon and Stone Harbor) to the east.

Christopher Leaming, who spelled his last name Leamyng, sailed from England for the colonies in 1670, landing in the Boston area, but later settling in Sag Harbor, East Hampton, Long Island.

In 1691, he left his family there and came to Cape May County. "Here he went a whaling in the proper seasons and at other times worked at the cooper's trade, which was his occupation." After his death in 1695, the property fell to his oldest son Thomas (1674-1723), who had joined him in the county in 1692.

Thomas Leaming wrote an accounting, or "anecdotes" of his life which were later copied by his nephew, Aaron Leaming Jr. into a large volume entitled *Surveys and Miscellaneous Deeds*. Found at the Cape May County Clerk's Office, this volume also includes surveys, early deeds, boundary dispute resolutions, and Aaron Leaming's own accounting of the history of the Leaming Family. Thomas Leaming, in his anecdotes, relates that "in 1706 I built my house" thereby giving a definitive date for the house's construction.

The Thomas Leaming House was not the first residence to be erected on the property, however. Thomas Leaming's detailed inventory of 1723 cites "one bed in ye west room of the new house" and the 1751 detailed inventory of his son Christopher mentions "the great room in the old house" and the "old house chamber." Since Thomas Leaming relates in his anecdotes that "in 1700 I lived at my own plantation," the earlier house was probably a simple, two-room structure offering modest housing until the larger dwelling was erected as his family increased in size.

Thomas Leaming, like his son, grandson, and most later owners, farmed the land with such crops as HAY, CORN, WHEAT, FLAX, RYE and TOBACCO. He also owned two slaves and raised cattle, sheep, oxen and horses. It is possible that he was a cooper, too, as his inventory lists cooper's tools which would have been an adjunct of his whaling.

On Thomas Leaming's death in 1723, the property was devised to Christopher Leaming II (1712-1751), Thomas' eldest son. Christopher died intestate and the land passed to his only child, Christopher III (1739 -1788) in 1751. During Christopher III's ownership, the size of the property increased from 204 to 330 acres with the addition of adjoining land containing "marsh and fisheries." Christopher III's will of 1787 divides the property between his sons, Humphrey and

Christopher IV, with Humphrey getting that half to the north which contained the Leaming House.

Humphrey Leaming Sr. (1780-1852) cultivated GRAIN, CORN, HAY and POTATOES, and raised cattle, sheep and hogs on the property. In 1831, he and a neighbor, Enoch Godfrey, sold a small parcel of land taken from both of their properties to the Asbury Church, located south of the Leaming House.

He also served as the county surrogate from 1831 until his death in 1852. Humphrey's will gave each of his five children one fifth of his estate. The farmstead was rented out until it was eventually divided in half, with Humphrey Leaming Jr. (1813-1892) receiving the northern half in 1865. This parcel comprised of 101 acres, was bisected by the present State Road Route 9 which runs roughly from north to south.

In 1865, Humphrey moved his family from Cape May City "to Townsend's Inlet, on the old Leaming farm and homestead, where he had spent his boyhood days." During his ownership, Humphrey and his wife sold a third-acre lot on the east side of Route 9 to their youngest daughter, Emma Leaming Kandle. After Humphrey Leaming Jr.'s death in 1892, the property passed to his daughter Annie Leaming (1853-1926). Annie was an eccentric spinster who taught music, sold produce from a truck farm on the property and mended "rail fences on the farm where she rented pasture for cows."

After Annie Leaming's death, the property was bought in 1927 from her administrator by Frederick M. Brodbeck. Brodbeck rented the farm for nearly 20 years, then sold it to F. Frank Leibig in 1948. Leibig, in turn, sold it to Margaret and Harry Colson in 1950.

The Colsons then sold the 50-acre portion on the west side of Route 9 containing the house, to Richard and Leota Hutton in 1952. The Huttons sold the house and its 50 acres in 1957 to the present owners, Jack and Emily Aprill. The Aprills sold approximately 30 acres, taken off the westernmost end, to the state for conservation purposes and created Leaming's Run Gardens in 1976.

The Thomas Leaming House, built in 1706 by whaler Thomas Leaming, is a material representation of the permanent settling of Cape May County which began in the late 18th century with the emigration of whalers like Thomas Leaming from New England.

During the first decades of the 18th century, he became one of the largest land owners in the county and served as a justice in the county courts from 1713 until his death in 1723.

As the county developed, albeit slowly in the early 1700s, Thomas Leaming gained prominence as one of the area's leaders. He was a Quaker, one of the few to settle in the lower half of the peninsula when most of that faith settled in the northern half. His nephew, Aaron Leaming Jr., recalled that the family was originally Presbyterian, but Thomas and his wife were zealous adherents to the Quaker faith. Thomas noted in his "anecdotes" that he was fined with the seizure of a horse worth 7 pounds because he would not train with the militia.

In 1713 he was commissioned as a justice of the peace and appointed to the several courts of Cape May County; in 1716 he was specially commissioned a judge of the Court of Common Pleas, recommissioned in 1721, and probably held that position until his death in 1723. At the time of his death, he owned more than 860 acres in Cape May County, making him one of the largest landholders at that time. Thomas Leaming, then, is significant as one of the first wave of pioneering whalers to settle and live permanently in Cape May County. In his later years, he amassed a large holding of land and, as a judge, held and esteemed position amongst his peers adjudicating laws early in the county's history.

Architecture

East Jersey Whaling families moved to the Cape May peninsula in the 1680s, completing a 17th century migration that had taken them from the British Isles to New England, to Long Island, and finally to East and West Jersey. The Leaming family was no exception. The Leamings' emigration from Long Island mirrors that of other Long Island families originally from England via New England, who relocated to Cape May County in the late 17th early 18th centuries—the Stites, Cresses, and Hands among them.

These early settlers to Cape May brought with them the building practices used in New England which reflected the 16th century East Anglia experience in building with timber. In the colonies, these practices were modified by physical conditions and practical concerns.

Seen in context, then, the Leaming House, with its heavy timber frame construction, significantly embodies and illustrates a method of construction characteristic of early Cape May County, but found rarely elsewhere in the state. Although heavy timber frame construction was just as commonplace in other New Jersey counties, few examples have survived. As originally built, the houses' two-room plan was atypical for the area, although its clapboard exterior, cedar shake roof, interior board sheathing, and exposed framing members are characteristic of this building type in the county.

Estimated to number less than two dozen by the New Jersey Historic Preservation Office, Cape May County's heavy timber frame structures, like the Leaming House, stand as significant examples which embody the architectural heritage and building traditions brought by the county's early settlers.

Epilogue
The Leaming Gravestones

Three gravestones deep in the woods across the street from our property marked the graves for Christopher Leaming II, Deborah Leaming Spicer, and the third is for their daughter Ester. After Christopher died, Deborah married Jacob Spicer; however in colonial days, the wife was buried with her first husband.

The gravestones were hidden and completely covered with HONEYSUCKLE and CAT BRIERS. I was very concerned about their safety. I felt the gravestones were works of art and should be cared for, especially since they were such an important part of the history of this property.

Once I found out about the gravestones, I wrote several times to the owner, asking permission to move the gravestones here to the homestead. The owner never answered any of my pleading letters and I felt that was the end of that.

However, one weekend while we were out of town, two young boys started a campfire in the woods. The blaze got out of control, setting the woods on fire. The fire company had to be called and also a bulldozer to make a fire line. The gravestones were almost hit and destroyed by the bulldozer.

I was really upset when I heard of this and decided to write again, this time to the owner's wife telling her of the fire and the danger to the gravestones. Responding, she refused to have the gravestones moved because of her religious beliefs. I was sad but resigned; I felt I had done the best I could to save them.

Then, a few years ago a strange thing happened concerning the gravestones. A woman who earlier told me she was from Indonesia had visited the gardens and then came back into the shop. She looked around for awhile and then said to me, "May I tell you something?"

"Please tell me," I said.

I thought she would tell me something about the gardens she thought might be improved. I am always eager to hear suggestions from our garden visitors about what they think might be a good idea, or work better, etc.

And then she said, "I saw the original owner of the property. He was a short man, dressed all in black and he had two small children with him."

"Ask him if it is okay with him if we move the gravestones," I said to her in a light-hearted way. She quickly put her hands to her temples, closed her eyes and appeared to be in a trance. A shiver ran down my spine and goose bumps covered my arms. In a minute or two she opened her eyes and said the property was for sale where the gravestones were. (It was true the property was for sale. How did she know this?) Then she told me that he said yes, it would be all right to move the gravestones to the homestead.

The property finally was sold last year and the new owners let us move the gravestones here to the homestead where they will be cared for and protected from harm.

Christopher Leaming II
December 31, 1751
In the 39th Year of His Age

Ester Leaming
March 17, 1749
In the 12th Year of Her Age

Deborah Leaming Spicer
February 27, 1784
In the 68th Year of Her Age

I feel my long quest to preserve and guard these artifacts has ended happily, and we are very grateful to the new owners for allowing us to move them here.

Emily Aprill